Chosen

Why Me?

MILTON VILLARREAL

ISBN 978-1-63630-716-9 (Paperback)
ISBN 978-1-63630-717-6 (Hardcover)
ISBN 978-1-63630-718-3 (Digital)

Covenant Books, Inc.
11661 Hwy 707
Murrells Inlet, SC 29576
www.covenantbooks.com

Contents

Acknowledgments

First of all, I want to thank God as it is because of him that I am alive to share this book with you. One of the things I struggle with is being able to concentrate and remember details from my past. Thanks be to God because he is good! He helped me remember and concentrate so this book could become a reality.

I want to thank my wife, Yendi, who has been a great blessing in my life and for being the ideal helper that Jesus had for me. She is a great woman, whom I admire very much for her wisdom and intelligence, but above all, for her perseverance and fear of God. When I was discouraged because God didn't answer as I expected or how I thought he should, she reminded me of God's promises over my life. When I didn't feel like writing or thought I had nothing to write, in those moments, she would encourage me to sit in front of the computer and seek God. And when I felt discouraged because of the lengthy process of writing a book, my beloved wife would remind me this book is God's project, not mine. And she is absolutely right!

I also want to thank my children, Yair and Marlon, for their support and their prayers. Yair has a noble and kind heart. Marlon has a faith that moves mountains.

Finally, I want to thank the pastors, staff, and entire team at International Christian Center (ICC) in Brownsville, Texas, my home church. ICC is where I made the most important decision of my life—that was to give my life to Jesus. God used ICC and its leaders to restore my marriage. Had I not been part of ICC, perhaps my story would be very different.

Introduction

This book contains part of my testimonies. I will specifically share times when I heard the voice of God—the times I obeyed and also the times I did not. As I wrote this book, I realized that God had been taking care of me. I began to wonder how he chose me to write this book. "Why me, Lord?" I asked. I thought, *Well, there certainly are others with better stories and testimonies than mine.* I realized that he chose me in spite of my limitations, and I am sure he has done the same with you. Think about it. Do you realize it? God has called us to bring hope to those who no longer have it. It doesn't matter what we may be going through, God can still use you.

> And they have defeated him by the blood of the Lamb and by their testimony. And they did not love their lives so much that they were afraid to die. (Revelation 12:11 NLT)

*(The way we can defeat the enemy is by
sharing our testimony to the world. Nobody
will take away or change my mind on what
Jesus has done in me and through me.)*

I've realized, and you too will have a chance to see, I have many limitations. But I've also realized God loves me in spite of my limitations. Not only does he loves me, he chose me. It is my desire that as you read this book, you too will realize that beyond your limitations, God has chosen you for his purpose.

I will also share experiences, revelations, and things that God has asked me to do or said to me. There are times when God asks us to do things, and we do not know if it is really him or our own emotions or desires. There are times we listen to the Holy Spirit who asks us to do things, which are not very difficult, such as helping someone out with $5.00 or paying for a stranger's meal. But what about when he asks you to give your car to someone you just met or forgive a debt of thousands of dollars or pray for a paralytic to be healed and to be able to walk, would you do it? You may wonder if that was God or the devil who is tempting you to do something outside your comfort zone. This has happened to me. In the next few pages, I will share with you my reaction in those situations and the outcome as in the scripture, "Declare His glory among the nations, His wonders among all peoples" (Psalm 96:3). That is what I will attempt to do in this book.

I started writing this book on Thursday, June 23, 2016. I couldn't sleep that night. It was 1:00 a.m. when the spirit of God told me to get up to write a book. And I kept hearing, "Book. Book. Book." I asked myself, "A book? For what? About what?" I wasn't sleepy, but I didn't want to get up either. I was very comfortable in bed. I then saw it was 2:00 a.m. and that's when I got up. I went to a room next to my bedroom, without making noise so as not to wake my wife up and sat in front of the computer. Then I said to the Lord, "Here I am. What am I going to write?"

He answered, "You will write about everything I have done for you and what I have revealed to you and the times that I have protected you."

As my fingers began to touch the keyboard, I didn't even realize that time was passing by. God was reminding me of things that happened when I was a child, and at the same time of the things he had done for me when I had a stroke (which I will tell you about later). By the time I saw the clock, it was already 3:30 a.m. I said, "Wow, this is great. I like this!" And that is how night after night I wrote this book. In the middle of the night, especially. Why at night you might ask? Because in the middle of the night, it is all very quiet and still. Some time ago, I heard someone preach that God speaks when it is quiet through whispers, just as he did to Elijah in 1 Kings 19. It was there where this adventure of writing a book began. Night after night, I kept writing this book.

After writing for nights, I suspended writing because I thought I had nothing else to write. It seemed as if God was no longer giving me revelation for the book. It was until May of this year (2019), at a men's conference, that he told me that this year I would finish the book. Even then, several months went by without writing. It was in August that I started to set the alarm at 5:45 a.m. to resume writing and finish what I had already started.

The Encounter

———————◉———————

Many times, I wondered why I had not done anything successful in my life. At least that is what I thought because I was only considering the professional and financial aspects of my life. I have an associate of network administration and a bachelor's degree in computer information systems. For more than eleven years, I struggled to get a job. When I applied for jobs that only required a high school diploma as the minimum qualification, my application was denied as I was overqualified.

On March 13, 2006, at the age of twenty-eight, I met Jesus. That day I had left work to eat with my friend Luis at lunchtime when, all of a sudden, I could not grasp what he was telling me. My right leg started to get numb, and my right hand did not respond properly. I couldn't raise my hand even to drink my soda. When Luis realized something was going on, he asked if I was okay. By that time, I could no longer coordinate my movements. I wanted to answer, "No!" by moving my head sideways, but I replied nodding my head, as if to say "Yes." So he kept on talking as if everything was fine. I got up from my chair and, as I could, threw away the unfinished food in the trash can that was near the exit. Then Luis got up as well and asked if we were leaving. I couldn't speak anymore. I remember that my right arm was no longer responding, and my right leg continued to weaken.

I did not understand what was happening to me. I was only twenty-eight years old and had always been a healthy man, very slim but healthy. When I got in the car, Luis told me that he would be driving because he saw that my right leg was not responding, not even to push the accelerator. Then I got up from the driver's seat and went to the passenger seat. As I sat and put my left leg in the car, I suddenly could no longer feel my right leg at all. All this happened very quickly. I remembered looking at Luis in the eyes, wanting to shout at him to do something because I didn't feel well, but I couldn't. Finally, Luis realized I needed medical assistance and went to call an ambulance. When he returned, he told me that the ambulance was already on its way. I started to vomit and then passed out.

When the paramedics arrived, they got me on the ambulance. The paramedics asked me questions, if I knew my name or where I was, and then I passed out again until we arrived at the hospital. To this day, I remember what happened in that ambulance on the way from the restaurant to the hospital. I saw a white light, bright as the sun, and I heard a voice that said, "Milton, your wife loves you, and everything will be okay." Although I had never heard that voice before that spoke to me with such authority, it gave me much peace.

When I woke up at the hospital, I remember seeing my wife crying and my son holding his mother's hand, somewhat frightened. I wanted to tell my wife what God had told me in the ambulance so she wouldn't worry, but I couldn't even speak anymore. I passed out again, and I woke up a few days later.

This time, it was different when I woke up. This time, perhaps because my brain was swollen by the massive bleeding that I had just experienced because of the stroke, I forgot what had happened; however, the peace that I felt was something I cannot explain. Although I could not speak or move the right side of my body, I felt calm. I had that peace his word speaks about in Philippians 4:7, "And the peace of God, which surpasses all understanding, will guard your hearts and minds through Christ Jesus."

(He will pour his spirit of peace over you.)

Later, my wife informed me that I had suffered a stroke and that was why I became ill. Even then, I was calm because I knew that God was going to restore all my movements and my speech because he had already told me so while in the ambulance. As the scripture states in Numbers 23:19, "God is not a man, that He should lie, nor a son of man, that He should repent. Has He said, and will He not do? Or has He spoken, and will He not make it good?"

And since then, God began to prepare me for His purpose, not mine.

> *(When God has given you a dream, a vision, or promised you something, he will do it. He will make a way; he will open the door because he is the way. He is a miracle worker.)*

Prior to...

A few months before I suffered the stroke, my wife and me were dealing with issues in our marriage. We were going through a marriage crisis. After so much insistence from my wife, we began to seek help from therapists, psychologists, and even a priest to counsel us. I didn't want anyone's help. It was as if I had a cover over my eyes that I didn't want anything with my wife. I thought that our marriage could not be fixed. I had been through so much that I didn't want to try to save our marriage. Boy, I was wrong!

During that time, my wife's cousin invited her to go to church. At the same time, a coworker of my wife would also invite her to church and speak to her about Jesus. My wife started going to church, the same church we are a part of today, International Christian Center. As our marriage was still in a crisis, it was recommended that a church couple would go to our house and pray for our marriage. That day, when the couple from church went to the house, I didn't want to see anyone. I'm sure they could tell how wrong I was because of my attitude and the things I said. The man looked at me and smiled, as if saying, "You don't know what you are saying, boy." He asked us if he could pray for us. I agreed, and he began to pray.

Yes, I thought I was a good husband because I didn't have bad habits, nor did I mistreat my wife or party with my friends. But in reality, I was not. I was not the husband of whom the Word of God speaks. I did not love my wife as Christ loves the church (Ephesians 5:25), nor did I comply with his instructions about marriage. However, at that time, I did not know that.

Since things did not improve between my wife and me, I decided to leave the house. I felt so hopeless that I thought there was nothing more that could be done for our marriage; no reason to try, except my child, Yair. Something inside of me knew that I was causing him great harm; his tears and his cries of desperation when he saw or knew that I was leaving the house every night hurt him because he did not want me to leave. When I left home, I went to my parent's house. I remember arriving at their house, and they were surprised to see me. They asked me what had happened. With tears in my eyes, I told them that Yendi and me had separated.

The next day, I went to work. I bought some tamales that day. At lunchtime, I only ate three tamales and put the rest away. I then went outside of the store to smoke a cigarette and saw two men at a distance. One of them approached me to ask for food.

I told him that I had tamales that I had not eaten. I went and got the tamales. When I returned, I gave him the tamales and noticed there were needle marks on his arms. When he realized that I was looking at him, he smiled and said, "I was a drug addict. I started smoking marijuana and then cocaine until I got to this, heroin." His friend had been the one who rescued him from drugs. He also began to tell me that he had a family that he missed a lot. That his greatest desire was to be able to return with his family, especially to know about his son and to play soccer with him since he had not seen him in a long time. He told me that the man he had met was going to take him with his wife and son because that was what he most longed for. He continued and said, "I know what's wrong with you. You are sad, but don't worry, everything will be okay." He walked away to where his friend was, then I lost sight of them, and I didn't see what direction they took or even where they went. At that time, I didn't know anything about the things of God. I knew and believed that there was a God but did not know the magnitude of his power, his love, or his grace. I realized that this man was someone special. Now I know he must have been an angel of God that showed up that day to bless me. As it says in Psalm 91:11, "For He shall *give His angels charge* over you, to keep you in all your ways" (emphasis added). Since our conversation, I was confused about the separation. His words made me realize that I was going through something very similar, and it seemed as if he knew about it.

*(God promised to be with you, to
keep you and protect you.)*

A few weeks later, I agreed to go to church with
my wife. I felt odd because I had never been to a
Christian church. The music made me feel out of
place, but it wasn't bad. I watched as people raised
their hands and others cried. Then I saw the pastor
got up on the platform to give a message. I will confess that on that very first time I went to church, I
made fun of the people at church and the way they
expressed their love for Jesus. I was so wrong. I then
went back to church with my wife, but only so she
would not say that I was not trying to save our
marriage.

We also started attending a couple's small group;
however, I would remain silent throughout the small
group. The leader of the group was the brother who
went to pray for us that day when I was very rude.
Even though we were going to church, to therapy
with a counselor, and to the small group, things
weren't getting better.

A few days later, my wife asked me to go on
vacation to spend time together and alone. I told her
that I couldn't; that I had to work and that, most
likely, wouldn't get the days off. But to my surprise,
that weekend I was off. I didn't want to go because
I already had other plans. My wife insisted so much
that I agreed to go.

We drove from Brownsville, Texas, to Monterrey,
Mexico—which is about a three-hour drive. I spent

most of my time ignoring my wife, to the extent that I ignored her most of the time we were in Monterrey. I told her we should get back home early because I felt that it was not working, that it was a waste of time, and I had to go to work. We drove back that night and arrived in Brownsville at 4:00 a.m. My wife asked me not to show up to work because I hadn't had much sleep. She asked me to stay with her, but I didn't want to. At 8:00 a.m., I got up and went to work. While I was at work, my wife was at home, crying out to God for me and for our marriage all morning. At lunchtime, I went out to have lunch with my friend. That's when I had the stroke.

When I was discharged from the hospital, I was transferred to a rehabilitation hospital to help me recover my movements and speech. I still didn't know, but the stroke had also affected my ability to write. Once at the rehabilitation hospital, I was giving it my all because I wanted to recover as soon as possible. While I was finishing therapy for the day, the neurologist who treated me for my stroke went to visit a patient at the same rehabilitation hospital. When my wife saw him, she told him that I was walking already. He could not believe it. This had been the same doctor who, in the emergency room, told my wife that the bleed in my brain had been so severe that he was not sure that I would live. He was so surprised to hear that I was walking that he asked my wife to take him to see me. When they arrived at the dining room where I was, the neurologist told me, "Milton, get up." So I stood up. He also asked me to walk, and I walked. He stood there with his mouth opened and said, "Milton, someone loves you very much up there because when I saw your MRI, you shouldn't be walking." Actually, he didn't think that I would survive the bleeding in my brain, but he was glad to see that I was doing much better. Now I know God has better plans for me as it is stated in Jeremiah 29:11, "'For I know the plans I have for you,' declares the Lord, 'plans to prosper you and not to harm you, plans to give you hope and a future.'"

(God's plans are way better than the ones we have. He is the creator of this world and created you and me. Don't you think his plans for our lives are way better?)

Jehovah Nissi

———————●———————

I remember that as a child, when I was around six years old, my family—my two older brothers, my dad, and my mom—would go buy groceries. At that time, we lived in Matamoros, Mexico, and went to Brownsville, Texas, to purchase our groceries. I was filled with joy every time we entered the supermarket because I liked sweets a lot, and there was candy that was not sold in Matamoros. I remembered a specific occasion when I was going to ask my dad to buy me a candy, but I saw he seemed bothered, so I put the candy in my pocket. On our way back home, I took candies in my hand quickly, and before anyone saw me, I shoved it in my mouth. Suddenly, I felt that the candy ball, which was quite large for a six-year-old boy, got stuck in my throat. My brothers realized that I was choking on the candy. One of them told my dad to stop the car because of what was happening to me. Dad parked quickly and started hitting me on my back so that I could expel the candy. At that moment, I felt so weak since I felt I could not breathe. My mom was very scared because she saw me turn blue. My dad took me and began to push against my esophagus. Finally, I was able to expel the candy, and I could breathe again.

Years later, at fourteen years old, I started cycling in my neighborhood. It was then that I met Arturo, Hugo, Juan, Little George, and three others. We rode our bikes at night, touring our neighborhood. The street where I lived was the street that divided the neighborhoods. On one of many nights, my friends and me were going back to my house when we were confronted by some not very friendly cyclers. These guys were those from the other neighborhood. They were troublemakers. They stole, did drugs, and always carried knives. When they saw us, they confronted us. They didn't want to be our friends and didn't like that we were going through "their" neighborhood. I realized that they were going to hurt one of us because one of them was holding a bat and another one pulled out a knife. That day, by chance, I was carrying a BB gun. I didn't normally carry a gun, but that day, I had it with me. I came out from behind my friends, holding the gun in my hand. You should have seen their faces when they saw that I had a gun. It was very funny! (Well, not at that moment, but it was later.) They backed up without hurting us. After the gun scare, they even asked us to gather the groups. Of course, we said no because we weren't troublemakers. My friends and me just rode our bikes for fun. Till this day, they never found out that the gun was only a BB gun.

On another occasion, I went to Juan's house, who lived on the very busy corner. I was on my bicycle, when suddenly, a passenger van ran over my bicycle. The rear tire passed over my left foot and shattered my bike. Everything happened so quickly that I didn't know what to think. I was obviously startled by what had happened, but at the same time, I was so surprised that nothing happened to me even after the van ran over my foot. My foot was fine! It reminds me of what the scripture says in Psalm 121:8, "The Lord shall preserve you're going out and your coming in from this time forth, and even forevermore."

(The Lord will keep you under his wings. He is your armor.)

There was also a time when I was riding my bike by myself, looking for my friends. We didn't have a specific place where we would meet, so we would go from one house to another, searching for each other. I started at Little George's house, but that night, my friends were not there. One of his brothers told me he was at Hugo's house. Hugo's house was at the other end of the neighborhood, where Little George lived. And there I was, on my way to look for my friends at Hugo's house. When I arrived at Hugo's house, his mother told me that my friends had already left to Juan's house. By that time, I had practically traveled the entire neighborhood on my bike in search of my friends. I went back to Juan's house, and they weren't there either. So I made my way to Arturo's house, and as I rode down the street, pedaling my bicycle, a car that was parked on the street suddenly and quickly reversed, even burning rubber, and ran me over. When the driver of the car realized that I was under the car, he was very frightened. My bike was in such bad shape that I couldn't ride it anymore. The front wheel got twisted, the rear tire was flat, the seat broke, and the bicycle's handlebars moved from their position in a way that I could no longer straighten them. He asked if I was okay. And to both of our surprise, I was. I got off the pavement without a single scratch. It was the hand of God that protected me that day.

When my wife and me started dating, I would go visit her. She lived in Brownsville, Texas, and me in Matamoros, Mexico. One night, as I was driving back home from visiting her, it began raining. I was going down the left lane, and there was no traffic that night; in fact, the street seemed to be vacant. Suddenly, I was hit from behind. Since I had my foot on the accelerator as I was rear-ended, instead of hitting the brake, I stepped on the accelerator with greater strength. My car began to slide to the left. It all happened very quickly. There were two restaurants in front of me, and I knew I was going to crash into them, so I had to react immediately. I don't know how, but I ended up right in between the two restaurants. In the middle of those two restaurants was a lamppost that fell on top of my car.

There was an employee at one of the restaurants who witnessed what happened. After a few seconds, he approached to make sure I was fine, because when the lamppost fell on my car, there were sparks from the electrical wires. He wanted to make sure I was not electrocuted and was okay.

At that time, I didn't know anything about God. I knew there was a God, but that's it. I didn't know about his power and how wonderful he is. Now I understand what verse 1 Peter 2:9 says: "But you are a chosen generation, a royal priesthood, a holy nation, His own special people, that you may proclaim the praises of Him who called you out of darkness into His marvelous light."

('Til the end of time we will be yours.)

After I recovered from the stroke, I promised the Lord that I would serve him by playing the guitar at the church. I was so grateful because he had saved my life and because he was healing me. God opened the doors so that I could serve him as part of the church's worship team.

One afternoon, I was on the expressway at about sixty-five miles per hour. I was on my way to church to practice with the worship team, when suddenly I passed out. In other words, I lost consciousness while traveling on a Brownsville, Texas, highway at sixty-five miles per hour to church from my house. Have you heard of spiritual warfare? Well, I was being attacked in a way that I had never experienced before. I remembered when I regained my senses, I was screaming. I shouted, "Jesus is my Lord! Jesus is my Savior! There is power in the name of Jesus!" Even unconscious, I knew who has the power.

I opened my eyes and looked around me. My car was parked in the parking lot of a commercial plaza on the frontage. Remember the scripture in Psalm 91:11, where it says, "For He shall give His angels charge over you, to keep you in all your ways"? God must have sent angels to drive my car that day from the expressway to that parking lot. I did not know what happened at that time; all I know is that it was not normal. I called my wife so she could go get me because I couldn't drive. I felt like I was not all there, as if I was being pressed from my head and very weak. My wife got there right away.

Once at home, I told my wife what I remembered about what had happened on the expressway. My wife knew that it was a spiritual attack, so she began to cast out the demons she believed were oppressing me—spirit of death and spirit of witchcraft. We know that Jesus has given us that authority as he says in Luke 9:1, "Then He called His twelve disciples together and *gave them power and authority over all demons,* and to cure diseases" (emphasis added). Although the spirits resisted and said they would not leave, they had no choice and were cast out because they could not stay. They have to submit to the authority and name of the one who already defeated them: Jesus.

(He has given you authority over everything on earth and under the earth and the heavens. Don't give up. Trust in him.)

After the deliverance, I felt better but not completely well. A few days later, I could not drive again. My wife says that I looked like a zombie and that's really how I felt—my eyes looked very small, as if I was very sleepy. Within a week, my wife called Pastor Mark, the demon slayer as he has been nicknamed by our congregation, to tell him what was happening to me and see what he suggested.

My wife told him what had happened to me, starting from the time I lost consciousness on the expressway. Pastor Mark told her it could be the generational spirit. My wife and mother-in-law started fasting and praying to cast the demon out of me on Sunday. My wife says that during the deliverance, the demon began to cry, wanting to make them believe that it was I who was crying, but my wife knows well how I cry and quickly knew that it was the devil trying to deceive them. They continued to battle against the devil until it left. In an instant, I felt good! It was like going from night to day. I recovered my strength and my focus—free at last.

Not too long ago, my wife and me were on the expressway in our hometown. We were going back home after running several errands. We were in a VW Jetta. I really liked that car because I would stretch out my arm and hug my wife without any inconvenience. That day, I was driving and was hugging my wife with my right arm and holding on to the steering wheel with my left. We were very happy, talking about the plans God has for us as a couple and for our family. In front of us, on the same lane, was a tall white van that did not allow me to see what was ahead. Suddenly, the van changed lanes quickly, and we realized that in our lane was a pickup truck about thirty feet from us, but only at about twenty miles per hour. The pickup at twenty, and me only a few feet back at sixty-five miles per hour. We were going to crash! My wife has a habit of saying, and sometimes shouting, "Jesus! Jesus! Jesus!" since a time she heard Pastor Carlos Anacondia share that his wife shouted "Jesus! Jesus! Jesus!" on one occasion when they almost crashed. Well, that's what my sweet wife did. She began to exclaim, "Jesus! Jesus! Jesus!" In that moment, I maneuvered the car with one hand, first to the right, but there was a car that was very close to our car, so we would have crashed, and then quickly to the left, without causing an accident on the expressway. We thanked God for saving us from a terrible accident.

Now I understand, after several years of knowing Jesus, why God took care of me even though I did not know him. There are times when we do not know our purpose in life, but we all have a purpose according to the scripture in Ephesians 4:11, "And He Himself gave some to be apostles, some prophets, some evangelists, and some pastors and teachers." He has given each of us different callings. Sometimes we do not know how to use or develop the gifts or things with which he provides us to do and what he has called us to do.

CHOSEN

(We all have a purpose and a calling.
What are you doing with yours?)

As I was editing this book, my wife and I real-ized that God had provided the necessary skills and tools to not only start it but also finish writing it. Just as David was given the ability to fight with the bear and the lion, just as God gave Joseph the ability to interpret dreams, and just as he gave Samson the strength to fight his enemies, he has also given me the ability to write this book. Sometimes, we don't realize that we have the tools in front of us or the people to help us with our dreams and projects. God has already given us the ability, the strength, and the tools. But our minds limit us; therefore, we don't focus on the tools and all that we need to accomplish our goals. We have been made to his image and like-ness; we can do anything we want. Have you heard of the saying, "If you have lemons make lemonade"? Well, you might have lemons right now but don't know how to make the lemonade.

In my case, God provided all the tools for me to write and publish this book. The desk where I am editing this book was a gift to my wife by her for-mer boss. Years later, my wife was given the antique leather chair, with wooden accents, that I am using. It's very comfortable, by the way! Also, at her job, she was given the computer on which she has been editing this book. Not only that, but God also pro-vided financially to publish my book. As I got quotes to publish my book, I realized it was very expensive.

I asked God, "God, how can I publish this book if I don't have the financial resources right know?" A couple of months later, we received money from the government, unexpectedly. It was like God was saying, "Hey, Milton, I'm the creator and owner of gold and silver." I can imagine him pulling out his wallet and asking, "How much do you need?"

Part of what God wants is for us to be obedient and trust him. If I had not obeyed that night, maybe this book would not have been written or would have taken longer to complete. Remember what happened to the Israelites in the desert? Just imagine waiting forty years to reach the desired goal.

God is Good

————————◙————————

At about twelve years old, my dad would take us to the Catholic church. I saw that Dad would kneel in front of the cross to ask God for things. I couldn't hear what he asked or prayed for, but one day, I told myself, *Well, if Dad can, so can I.* Therefore, I began to pray. First, I prayed for my family, for me to do well in school, and since it was in, I even asked for a Nintendo. When I did not do my homework, I prayed the Our Father, and although it was rare, the teacher would forget to pick up the homework that day. At school, there was a teacher standing at the main entrance gate, which he shut right at 7:00 a.m., not a second later. When we were running late, I remembered the Our Father and prayed again. Now I realized that God knew about my concerns and anguish. Maybe I didn't ask for it in detail as I do now, but he knew what I needed, and since then, he helped me.

Well, going back to the Nintendo request I made to God at church, there was a bingo at school. They started off handing out small prizes, but we didn't win any. As usual, they left the best prizes until the end.

The last three were the big prizes. I then remembered the Our Father and my prayer at church. I began to pray the Our Father again because I wanted to win. I needed one number to win. And then, I heard the number I had intensely longed for was called out. I shouted loudly, "Bingo!" My heart was beating so fast with joy I thought it was going to come out of my chest. The prize was 1,000 Mexican pesos. God had done it again. I gave half of the prize to my mom and kept the other half to buy the Nintendo. Now I realize that God truly knows the desires of our heart.

> There is a time for everything, and a season for every activity under the heavens. (Ecclesiastes 3:1)

(Yes, there is a time and season for everything. Enjoy your season and wait for the next season.)

I know that God's timing is perfect, and I look forward to that time when my dad stops drinking alcohol completely. There was a time when I asked God specifically for my dad. I'd pray day and night for him. I told him, "If my dad gives his life to Christ first, my mother and my brothers will see the change in him, and then they will believe that there is a God who can transform hearts." One day, I heard a preaching about prayer where the preacher said that we should not worry about anything; that God had already heard our prayer, and that we just needed to thank God for having answered the prayer. That day, I told God that I was tired of praying for the same thing, but that I would be grateful as if he had already answered it, even if my eyes had not yet seen it. Sunday came, and we went to church. I was praising my Lord in the sanctuary, when out of nowhere, someone grabbed my ribs from behind—it was my dad. What a pleasant surprise I got that day! I began to praise God with greater joy. Sometime later, Dad took my mom to church. The two have already received Jesus. I believed in him, and I still believe. Now, I thank him for the rest of my family because I know that one day, they, too, will come to the feet of Jesus.

God has always been with me and my family. Why do I say this? When I had the stroke, I lost my job. I was about to finish my associates in network administration. When my teachers found out about what had happened to me, they did not hesitate to welcome me back to finish my degree. They knew that I was struggling to focus as a result of the stroke and would help me a lot. When we were asked to work on projects in groups, my teachers would let my group know what had happened to me, and the members of my group would support me as well. When I graduated with my associates, I hoped I could work and make some money. Unfortunately, there were times I couldn't even make the interview process.

Since I could not find a job, I decided to go back to school. I thought maybe the associates was not enough. I enrolled at the local university and started to struggle again. As a result of the stroke, it was very difficult for me to articulate and express my thoughts and ideas. I would lose focus very easily. For example, if I heard the neighbor's lawn mower or if someone was listening to music that was very loud, I could not concentrate, and I couldn't continue with my tasks. I stuttered and would quickly grow weary. In fact, because of that, after the stroke, I was considered disabled for years. I heard the university had a program for students with disabilities. I signed up to be part of the program. Several were summoned for an orientation. When I entered that room, I felt so blessed because what I was going through didn't compare to the disabilities or limitations that some of the other students there were going through. Seeing the condition of others made me want to leave. I felt I was taking advantage of the program since it did not look like I had any physical disabilities.

We took some tests to evaluate us and decide if we were qualified for the program and to determine where we were and how much help we needed. To my surprise, I was one of those chosen to be in the program; although while I was taking the tests, I began to think they would realize that my condition was not as bad as everyone else who was there and would not get a spot. I was wrong. Even though I did not understand at the time, I now realized that everything was planned by God, even to every small detail. That program opened the doors for me to go to the promised land. I will tell you about that later.

After I graduated from college, I was contacted by a program representative to offer me an internship in Dallas that summer. Around the same time, I also received a job offer in Brownsville, but I didn't take the job. I don't remember if I didn't take the offer because of the pay they were offering me, or that, in fact, my spirit had already decided to take the offer in Dallas. I now had a job, but the question was where would I live while working as an intern. Several options came up. I knew I had an uncle living in Denton, but his house was about an hour away from the company where I would be working at. I also thought about my cousin Miguel. He lived in Grand Prairie at the time, which was about a twenty-minute drive from work. I sent my cousin Miguel a message. He quickly answered me and didn't even hesitate to offer me his house. When we were kids, our families were very close. I remember that our families would get together every weekend and play loteria, soccer, basketball, and baseball. When I told my wife that my cousin had offered me to stay at his house, she could not believe it since it had been several years since Miguel had moved to Grand Prairie, and since he moved, we had not seen each other. Not only that, my cousin was now married, with a wife and kids, and I didn't even know them. My wife was very happy because I would not have to live by myself or have to rent an apartment in Dallas since that would have been a very big expense for us at that time.

Living with my cousin and his family was a blessing to me. Griselda, my cousin's wife, and their children welcomed me as if they already knew me. There were times when Gris would even cook food for me to take to work. There I met Evelyn, a little girl whom I love very much to this day. She is Gris's daughter. Shortly after living with them, I had the opportunity to share with Evelyn about God. We even had our small group. She invited her friends from the block, and every day from 6:00 p.m., I shared the Word of God with them at the dining-room table. I was also able to share Jesus with my cousin's wife.

Now I understand that I was not there by coincidence. The Lord commands us to go and preach the gospel as it is written in Mark 16:15. He said to them, "Go into all the world and preach the gospel to all creation."

Then, as days went by, I felt my spirit telling me to start looking for a church. It was like hungry to get connected to a local church. One day, on my way to work, I saw a small church and decided to go visit. When I entered, everyone looked at me like they weren't expecting new people. They looked at me as if I was a stranger, and I really felt that way. I guess they had not had visitors in a long time. I sat near the entrance door, but an usher asked me to move to a pew he had already chosen for me. I had no problem obeying the usher, and I moved right away. It was about forty-five minutes of worship and then the sermon.

I was chewing gum when an usher approached me and handed me a small piece of paper. The paper read, "Please place your gum in this paper." When I did, he approached me again to ask for the paper and throw it in the trash. I know that the Bible doesn't say anything about chewing gum at church, but I do understand that we must respect the church. Unfortunately, I felt very uncomfortable, and I decided to leave before the service ended. I think that if I were in a similar situation today, out of respect, I would stay until the end. Well, the scripture says in Romans 13:1, "Everyone must submit to governing authorities. For all authority comes from God, and those in positions of authority have been placed there by God." Now, honoring and submitting to authority has become something very important in my life. If it is important to God, it must also be important to us.

*(Submission is not easy, but once you
do it, God will raise you up.)*

Back then, I didn't understand why I had had such an experience. What happened is I let my desires and convenience guide me to that church, but not the Holy Spirit. There are times when we allow our flesh guide us to satisfy our needs, instead of seeking God's guidance.

When my internship was over, I told my cousin and his family that I had to go back home with my wife and children and thanked them for opening the doors of their home to me. They didn't want me to leave; they wanted to adopt me. I remembered that Saturday that I was going to return home, I woke up early because it's an eight-hour drive. I didn't want to wake them up. I also grew very fond of them and assured them that I would visit them more often. It has been that way. Since my internship ended, my family and I tried to visit them once a year, and sometimes even more than that.

Several years ago, a sermon of Pastor Morris of the Gateway Church was played at our church. It was about putting God first in every area of our lives, including finances. We then searched him up and began watching his messages online. As time went by, we went to visit Miguel and his family. My wife and I had planned to go to Gateway Church since we would already be in that area. While at my cousin's house, we learned that Gateway Church has a campus in Grand Prairie, not far from my cousin's house. On Saturday afternoon, I told my cousin that my family and me were going to church on Sunday and asked if they would like to join us. They did not regularly attend church at that time. He said yes without hesitation. We were so happy. We woke up early on Sunday to have breakfast and got ready to go to church. When we entered the sanctuary, I felt the presence of the Holy Spirit very strong. My cousin felt the same. His wife and children liked the church very much, so much so that they continued to attend. My cousin and his whole family are now saved and members of Gateway Church.

Obedience

———————◉———————

> Pay attention to him and
> listen to what he says. Do not
> rebel against him; he will not
> forgive your rebellion, since my
> Name is in him.
>
> —Exodus 23:21

*(Mountains will move when you stay still
and keep quiet. You will hear his voice.)*

Child in a Wheelchair

For years now, my family and I attended church
regularly. Several years ago, when my children were
younger, we went to church as we did every Sunday.
Upon arrival, I went to register my children at
Sunday school. Since we arrived early, the doors of
the children's department were still closed, so we had
to wait in the hall for a few minutes. We were waiting
when a lady walked in with her young daughter in a
wheelchair. There was an awkward silence for a few

seconds, and then I heard a voice that said, "Tell her to get up from the chair." I turned to look at my son and asked, "What did you say?"

"Nothing," he answered.

It happened again. I heard the voice say, "Tell her to get up from the chair."

I would like to tell you that I did and that the little girl got up, but I didn't and she didn't. I was afraid to do it because I thought it was just me. These were moments of an internal battle. I thought if I tell her to get up and she doesn't, then what? The doors opened so we could register the children to go to their respective classrooms. I then went to the sanctuary, but with a great sadness, because in disobeying God, I had grieved the Holy Spirit. During worship, I asked God to forgive me for not obeying him. In fact, I left the sanctuary to look for the little girl throughout the church, but I didn't find her. I felt so bad. I asked God to give me another chance. Since then, I tried to be more sensitive to his voice and the instructions of the Holy Spirit.

Medicated Child

One day, God spoke to me through a dream about a boy who was taking pills prescribed by a doctor; however, these pills were hurting him instead of helping. The pills had been prescribed to help him with his anxiety attacks and lack of concentration. I remember very clearly what he said to me. "Tell them that I,

God, sent you so that they will stop giving their son that pill which is hurting him." So I had a talk with the Lord about what he was asking me to do because I didn't know how the boy's parents would take it. Have you ever done that? Try to get God to change his mind about something he's already instructed? Well, I did. I said, "Lord, why don't you reveal it to them yourself since they are also your children?" He did not answer, and I knew that I would have to be the one to tell them. Even then, I talked to my wife about it. She advised me to obey God, to deliver the message, and it would be up to the boy's parents to decide whether they accept it or not. Well, the next day, I prayed to build myself up with courage. I knew the Lord would be with me, just as he promised in Joshua 1:9, "Have I not commanded you? Be strong and of good courage; do not be afraid, nor be dismayed, for the Lord your God is with you wherever you go."

(He is the God almighty that would do anything for you. Please do not be dismayed.)

When I arrived at their house, I began to pray before getting out of the car. The boy's mother answered the door. I said, "God sent me to tell you to stop giving your son a pill that is hurting him." The expression on her face changed for a moment. I'm sure she did not know what to think about what I had just said. Can you imagine? Someone comes to your house and you think he is visiting, however, he tells you that a pill you are giving your child is hurting him instead of helping him? Not only that, but it is God who is telling you this. I believe that anyone could have been thrown off guard for a bit in that situation. I told her that the Lord had also shown me the color and size of the pill. She got up from where she was sitting and went to the kitchen, while I waited in the living room. She came back with all the pills her son was taking. She began to take one pill from each bottle. I was so amazed to see that one of those pills was exactly what God had shown me in the dream—small, oval-shaped, and blue. I pointed out the pill to her. She told me that she was going to ask the doctor about the side effects of that pill, and if it was something, she could stop giving her son. I told her that I had delivered the message; that was my assignment. I don't even know if they stopped giving the boy the pill, but I trust what the Word says in Romans 10:11, "For the Scripture says, 'Whoever believes on Him will not be put to shame.'"

*(God always has your back, just
trust on him and believe.)*

The Boss

I had been working approximately two weeks for a utility company in the auto-maintenance department, when the Lord asked me to give my boss a scripture. Can you imagine, my boss! I was the new guy. At that time, I was reading the story of Gideon, so I thought to myself, *If Gideon asked God for three signs to make sure that it was God who spoke to him, I'm sure I can do the same.* What I like about the story is that Gideon was specific in the signs he asked God for, and God answered him. So I did the same and was also specific when asking for the signs. The first sign I asked for was that my boss would call me on the phone. As soon as I finished praying for the sign, my phone rang. Who do you think it was? That's right! It was my boss. He asked if I had something for him. I said no as I was in shock.

Then he asked me again, "Are you sure you don't have anything for me?"

I again replied no. He told me it was fine and hung up. After we hung up, I was speechless for God had answered my request for the first sign. Even then, I was not at all convinced. The truth is, I was scared. I didn't know how Tom, my boss, would respond. Nor did I know the company's policies. In addition, I had barely been with the company for two weeks after years of unemployment, so I didn't want to put my job at risk. Then I thought of Gideon again and asked God for another sign. The sign I asked for was the same, that my boss would call me and ask the same thing. To my surprise, the phone rang again. Yes, it was my boss asking if I had something for him. I was stunned. I didn't know what to do except answer, "No." He told me it was fine and hung up. I asked God for forgiveness and asked for one last sign. This time, I asked my boss would come to my office and ask me the same thing. Having just finished praying for the third sign, my boss walked into my office. He asked me again if I had something for him, but this time, he told me that something had taken him to my office. I again answered no. He then went back to his office, and I was beyond words. God had come through! He gave me the three signs exactly how I asked for them, so it was up to me to do what God had instructed me to do. I got up from my chair and went to Tom's office. I gave him a small piece of paper where I had written the scripture God gave me for him. What he did next left me with my mouth open, for he quickly turned to his bookcase and pulled out a Bible he had in his office. I had never before seen a Bible in his office—didn't know he had one. He told me it was fine and that I could leave. At lunchtime, I was eating and chatting with my coworkers when Tom entered the dining room. My coworkers left and only Tom and me stayed in the dining room. He was crying as he asked me how I knew that this was the answer he needed since he had been praying for God to give him an answer, to guide him to make a decision. I told him that I did not know; that it was the Holy Spirit. I shared with him it was not easy and told him about the three signs I asked God for to confirm that it wasn't something I was making up. Then he asked me what church I went to, and I told him International Christian Center. It turns out that we were both going to the same church but different services. I went to the Spanish service, and he to the English service. I shared with him my testimony about the stroke and how God healed me. In just a few months, we became very good friends. I was also able to earn both Tom's and my fellow workers' respect.

240SX

I had a car that I liked very much. It was a red Nissan 240SX two-door sports car, with sunroof and manual transmission. I liked it so much that I thought I would keep it and not sell it. My dream with that car was to keep it until it became a classic or until I reached eighty years of age, and one day, give it to either one of my children or one of my grandchildren.

There was a time when my sister-in-law and her family lived in an apartment attached to the house where my family and me live. As time went by, my sister-in-law and her family moved out, and the apartment was left unoccupied. We knew a young girl with her two babies who was struggling to find a place to live. My wife and me prayed and decided to offer Tere[1] to stay in the apartment that my sister-in-law had inhabited. It was small but big enough for her and her girls. When we gave her the news, she was filled with joy.

At that time, she worked cleaning houses to support her babies. She is a very hardworking woman, and nothing is too difficult for her. One day, she sur-

---

[1]   Tere is a fictitious name to maintain the privacy of her identity.

prised us. She told us that her girls' father wanted to come live with her and the girls. She asked us if he could live in the apartment with her and their girls for a while. We did not think it was a problem since, after all, he was the father of the girls, and it seemed responsible on his part to want to take care of his daughters and provide for his family.

As time went by, we learned he could not find a job. They were also struggling with transportation since they did not have a car. At that time, we had three cars. One of those was my 240SX, which I would only drive occasionally. I remember very well, one day, that God asked me to give them the 240SX. I began to rebuke that voice because I was sure that could not come from God since God knew how much I liked that car. Has that ever happened to you? Has God ever asked you for something you don't want to give up? I can now advise you to trust God and do it. Otherwise, you may still lose it. However, when you obey, you are giving God an opportunity to bless you. But at the time, I didn't want to do it! It was my favorite car. How was I going to give it to someone I had just met? I talked to my wife about that. My wife has a very generous heart, so she was very happy. She told me to obey God. We invited them to dinner one night at our house. At the end of dinner, I told them that God had a gift for them. I gave them the car keys and the signed title so they could change owner-ship. Tere cried. Carlos,[2] the girls' dad, was also very

---

[2]   Carlos is a fictitious name to maintain the privacy of his identity.

happy. We explained that it was something that God wanted to give to them, and we wanted to obey him.

A few weeks went by, and Carlos still couldn't find a job. One day, I was locked out of my house and had to get back in. I was trying to open the front door with screwdrivers and credit cards, just as I'd seen in movies. Carlos got there and offered to help. He told me that the only way to open the door was to break part of the doorframe, so we did. After a few minutes, we managed to open the door and enter my house, but I did not fix the doorframe.

Later, he asked me if I could burn songs on a CD for him. We walked to my office, looking for music on the computer. I then pulled out my laptop from the office closet to find more songs I had on that computer. I had just bought that laptop a month prior. My wife called, asking me to run an errand. I don't remember why, but I had to go in a hurry. I told Carlos that I had to leave, but we would continue to search for songs later. A few days later, while I was out of the house, he called me on the phone, asking me where I was at and if I was going back to the house to finish recording the CD. I thought his question was odd since it was not something urgent, and it could wait until I got home but didn't think much of it.

A few days later, he arrived at the house with a new car sound system, with a value of approximately $1,000. He showed me the sound system and asked if I liked the way it sounded. It was one of those stereos with large removable screen, with illuminated buttons and large speakers, loud enough for the entire block to hear his music. But the truth is, I questioned how he could afford such an expensive audio system without a job. I didn't wonder very long and asked him where he got it from. He told me that his uncle had bought it for him, and that when he had money, he would pay for it.

A few days later, my wife was looking for her laptop but couldn't find it. Since she didn't find it, she asked for my laptop. She then went to my office and opened the closet door, looking for my laptop. When she opened the backpack to pull out my laptop, she realized that it was not there. She shouted from the office that the laptop was missing. By the time I got to the office, my wife was already looking for the laptop on my desk and under my desk and in a bookcase that was also there. I also looked for it everywhere, but we couldn't find it. Then my wife asked when I used it last. I quickly remember that it was when I was with Carlos, trying to burn a CD. I told my wife about what happened. We realized that we were missing more items. We concluded that we were missing three laptops, a video camera, and some of my wife's jewelry. My wife started crying. By that time, I was already very angry. Something like this had never happened to us. Someone had entered our home while we were gone and taken things that did not belong to them.

As much as I didn't want to think that it had been Carlos, whom I had given my favorite car to so that he and his family did not have to walk, everything pointed to him. I wanted to go and set him straight, but my wife asked me to calm down, that it was not good for me to get angry like that; besides, we weren't sure it would have been him. *Well, who else?* He knew exactly where the laptop was; he knew how to open the door to my house without a key; he knew that I was not home and at what time I would return. I went to confront him, and of course, he denied it. So we called Tere, who wasn't home at the time. She arrived a few minutes later to see what was going on. When she arrived, she spoke with him, but he continued to deny it hadn't been him. Tere then talked to Carlos's sister, and she confirmed it. He had exchanged some computers for the car sound system. Can you believe it? He went into our house to rob. When she told me that, I wanted to call the police. But I heard a voice that said, "Don't do anything about it." I turned to look at my wife and said, "Why not? Didn't you just hear what he did? He robbed us!" My wife looked at me with confusion on her face and told me that she hadn't said anything. I knew then it was the Lord, and a peace came over me. And so it was, I did not press charges against Carlos. I told Carlos he had to leave. I didn't want him to live there anymore. The next morning, Tere went to the house to apologize for what had happened. She wanted to give us back the car because she said it was not right to keep it after what Carlos had done. She was so embarrassed. I told her to keep the car, but she insisted on returning it for me to buy another computer. After much insistence, I accepted.

Sometime later, I learned that Carlos continued with bad habits until he went to prison. The last thing I heard was that he had been sentenced to ten years for kidnapping. I wish him no harm. Now I know that there are times when we fall so low because of our own bad decisions that all we have left is to look up. I hope that happened to Carlos. That where he is, he has found Jesus.

I have learned that when someone hurts us, it is best not to do anything. Let God handle it because he has said, "It is mine to avenge; I will repay. In due time their foot will slip; their day of disaster is near and their doom rushes upon them" (Deuteronomy 32:35).

(Be still and know that he is God.
He will fight for you.)

The Resignation

After the stroke I suffered in 2006, I was unemployed for about eleven years, with the exception of the months I was in Dallas working as an intern and the four months I worked at the utility company with Tom. I am a man with a lot of patience. But after so much study, employment applications, and failed interviews, I became impatient. As I told you before, I went to school and graduated with an associates in network administration. I wanted to provide for my family as I should but simply could not after the stroke. Seeing that I couldn't find a job, I decided to go back to the university to obtain a bachelor's in computer information systems.

I spent many of those years in which I did not work getting to know God. Little by little, I learned that God is pleased that we spend time with him, when we seek him wholeheartedly. Although we had to make ends meet with my wife's salary and my disability check, we always had enough to pay all our expenses. There was always food on our table, and everything we needed. God provided for everything: from gas for the car to sweet bread for my cravings. But I was like the Israelites. I wanted more than just the everyday manna. One day, when I was already pretty desperate, I asked God why I couldn't find a job. I was frustrated, indebted with credit cards and student loans. He said, "Milton, you chose to study to fix computers, but I chose you to fix people with my grace." I got chills because when I decided to get an education in technology, I didn't ask God for direction as I didn't know him.

The very next day, I received an e-mail regarding a job. When I read it, I realized that it was to work for a company that subcontracted for Apple. I could not believe it! I looked up, as if God were in the ceiling of my bedroom, and asked, "Should I apply?" I clearly heard in his answer, a tone of frustration, almost annoyed by my insistence, "Well, apply." Let me say something. It's not that God didn't want me to have a job; however, God taught me things during that season of unemployment that I would not have learned had I been working. So I applied, and two days later, I was called for an interview. I had to take a test to evaluate my knowledge in connection with phones. I passed it, and the following week, they called to forward me the equipment so that I could start working as soon as possible.

I don't know if you've ever waited for years for something you think you need, and it just doesn't come. For eleven years, I couldn't get a job and believed that's what I needed. God is so merciful and gracious that even when he is not in approval of our decisions, he, like the good father that he is, will be there for us. I don't know what you might be waiting for, but I encourage you, trust in the Lord for he is in control. Trust his timing too, although this is pretty difficult; you don't want to arrive early and not be ready, but you also don't want to arrive late and miss out.

I was doing so well that after six months, my supervisor recommended I work at one of the departments that troubleshoot computers. I got a raise and a promotion. I was very happy! I liked my job so much that I came to think that I was going to retire from there. One day, God gave me the opportunity to minister to a coworker by sharing my testimony. We had previously had a team meeting. There, I talked a little about my faith in Jesus. She had gone through the same as me, a stroke, so she was struggling to concentrate as well. I told her that I believed God had healed me so much that I even stopped taking the medicine to prevent epileptic seizures, which

I had taken for years. (I am not a doctor; therefore, I cannot give you advice about your health, but I know one who is a healer, and I am sharing what he did for me.) I prayed for her. I asked her if she wanted to receive Jesus as her Savior, and she said she had already received him. She had.

A couple of weeks later, a leadership program, Next Level, was offered at church. It is a two-year program to develop leaders and give the opportunity to those who would like to work in the ministry to get an idea of what that is like. That program caught my attention because it is a development and a preparation for ministry. My wife was not very excited about taking the course, but since I was going to take it, she also signed up as to show her support. I was off from work on Mondays, which happen to be the day the Next Level classes were scheduled, so it worked perfectly for us.

Within a few weeks, there were changes in my job. My schedule was changed from morning to afternoon. Unfortunately, that would complicate my attendance on Mondays to the Next Level. Not only that, at that time, we had a couples' small group on Fridays, and I had to prepare.

The same week, my schedule changed. I heard God say, "It is time."

I asked, "Time for what?"

Then he replied, "It is time for you to resign from your job."

How was I to quit my job when I had just been promoted? Besides, I really liked my job. So again, I disobeyed.

A few days went by, and things at work weren't going well, so much that even customers were getting upset at me. At the end of the week, I was already very stressed out about work. I was also stressed out because we had the couples' small group that night, but I had nothing to share. Usually, when I spent time with God, he would tell me what he wanted me to share with the couples because he, better than me, knew what they were going through.

There was a time when he gave me the lesson for our couples' small group. The instructions were to write situations that couples deal with regularly. The day that I had the small group, the other couples, my wife and me were sitting in the living room at my house. I pulled out a jar with the little pieces of paper I had already folded, where I had written what God had told me. I asked each couple to take a piece of paper from the jar and told them not to open it yet. I started with the teaching on love according to the Word of God as follows:

> Love is patient, love is kind. It does not envy, it does not boast, it is not proud. It does not dishonor others, it is not self-seeking, it is not easily angered, it keeps no record of wrongs. Love does not delight in

evil but rejoices with the truth.
It always protects, always trusts,
always hopes, always perseveres.
(1 Corinthians 13: 4–7)

(All you need is love, nothing else, because he is love.)

Then I asked each couple to open the piece of paper they had taken. When they began to read their papers, we were all amazed at what their paper said as it contained situations that they, themselves, were going through or had been through. There were confessions and healing. Just what everybody needed.

A few weeks later, I called my wife at noon on the phone to ask for prayer because I did not have the teaching for small group that night. My wife was surprised but prayed for me. In the afternoon, when she arrived home from work, she noticed I was not well, and it was because I didn't feel at peace. She asked what was going on with me because it had been days. She could recognize I was uneasy. I told her that I didn't have the teaching for that night; that God had not spoken to me. She asked if I was being disobedient. I had no choice but to confess that God had asked me to quit my job. Without hesitating, she said, "What are you waiting for? You need to obey and resign."

I did not want to resign.

After so many years without a job, I finally felt useful. I felt that I was contributing financially to my family. Our finances were doing better; with both my wife and me working, we had more money. Besides, what if it wasn't God speaking?

Well, again, like Gideon, I wanted to make sure that it was really God who had spoken to me. The first sign I asked him for was to give me the teaching for that night. The second sign was that someone from the group specifically ask me, "Brother Milton, are you not working anymore?" The third, I left it up to him. He immediately gave me the teaching in about thirty minutes. It usually took me several days to prepare the teaching. It was now small-group time. I shared the teaching as I believed God had given it to me. Then we had dinner, and at dinner, one of the small-group members asked me, "Brother Milton, are you not working anymore?" By that time, I had already told my wife all about the agreement I had made with God. When the brother asked me the question, we both turned to see each other and were in awe.

Once we were done with the small group and all the couples had left, my wife and I began to analyze what had happened during the group to see how we could improve and help the couples. And of course, we also spoke about the signs. As we talked about the signs, my wife asked if I was now going to obey God. She continued telling me I should call work as soon as I get up the next morning, talk with my supervisor, and resign. I reminded her that I was still waiting for one more sign. We prayed to ask God to speak to us, to give us that sign, either through a message, a dream, or through his Word.

The next day, I got up. I first thanked God for my job and for the opportunity to minister to a fellow worker. Then I started to get ready for work. Well, to "go" work was more of an expression since I worked from home. So it was a matter of getting ready, eating something, and locking myself in my little office. My wife woke up right away and asked if God had already given me the third sign, or if I had dreamed something about work. I said no, a bit puzzled. But she, with a smile on her face, said, "Well, he did to me!" She grabbed her Bible and read the following:

> So it was, as the multitude pressed about Him to hear the word of God, that He stood by the Lake of Gennesaret, and saw two boats standing by the lake; but the fishermen had gone from them and were washing their nets. Then He got into one of the boats, which was Simon's, and asked him to put out a little from the land. And He sat down and taught the multitudes from the boat.
>
> When He had stopped speaking, He said to Simon, "Launch out into the deep and let down your nets for a catch."
>
> But Simon answered and said to Him, "Master, we have

toiled all night and caught nothing; nevertheless at Your word I will let down the net." And when they had done this, they caught a great number of fish, and their net was breaking. So, they signaled to their partners in the other boat to come and help them. And they came and filled both the boats, so that they began to sink. When Simon Peter saw it, he fell down at Jesus' knees, saying, "Depart from me, for I am a sinful man, O Lord!"

For he and all who were with him were astonished at the catch of fish which they had taken; and so also were James and John, the sons of Zebedee, who were partners with Simon. And Jesus said to Simon, "Do not be afraid. From now on you will catch men." So, when they had brought their boats to land, they forsook all and followed Him. (Luke 5:1–11 NKJV)

(You have a purpose. If you don't know what it is, ask God and he will reveal it to you. Just dwell in his presence.)

My wife is not only a woman who loves the Lord, but also loves his Word and enjoys teaching it very much. So, there on our bed, she began to explain to me why she believed that God had given her that passage. Jesus showed the disciples that he could do things that they, with all their effort and experience, could not achieve on their own. God had already shown that to me as well. He also told them that they would now catch men. Obviously, for that, they would have to follow Jesus and leave fishing, their jobs. My wife explained to me that Jesus did not ask everyone who believed in him to leave their jobs, but only those who he wanted to have close to him to disciple and use in a unique way. Then she told me, "That is why the Lord is asking you to quit your job." I also realized that God, just like he did with Peter, prepared me for the season without a job.

Jesus told the fishermen to throw the net to fish. What happened next was miraculous. There were so many fish in the nets that they began to break, two boats were filled with fish, and they began to sink. This miraculous fishing could have created resources for the families of the disciples who were there and now followed Jesus, so they would not have to worry about their well-being. In my case, while I worked, we were able to prepare for what was coming even when I didn't know it. A few months before God asked me to resign, he told me, "Fill your barns." We began to make the necessary adjustments in our finances for that. We cleared out a room in the house to turn it into a small storage. We also bought a freezer to freeze food. In those months, God gave my wife wisdom to coupon. Before long, our small storage was filled with all sorts of necessary items.

Well, going back to what God asked me to do. As soon as my wife finished explaining to me what God put in her heart, I called my supervisor and told him that I was no longer going to work with the company. He was surprised and asked me why. I let him know it was for personal reasons. He asked me if someone from the company had mistreated me or said something that made me want to quit. At that moment, God said, "Tell him why you are resigning." I thought about it for a moment. I asked myself, *How am I going to tell him? What if he doesn't believe me? What if he thinks I'm crazy?* Again, I heard the Lord say, "Tell him why you are resigning." Then I told my supervisor the reason for my resignation. His answer surprised me. He told me that he admired my faith, that he was not a believer but advised me to obey. Even then, he wanted to give me five days of vacation in case I changed my mind and wanted to return to work. I liked his kind gesture, but there was not turning back.

Mechanical Bull

There was a time when my wife and I wanted a business. We wanted a party hall for special events, such as birthday parties, weddings, and graduations— among others. We began to look at the party halls that were already in the city, and the truth is, there were already a lot. We began to think what we could bring to the city in that space that was unique and would attract customers. It had to be something that caught people's eye and set us apart from the competition.

We kept checking out party halls in the area. We even visited several of them to obtain information about what they offered and their prices. Most of these party halls had inflatables and playgrounds as their main attraction, only one had a small train. We wanted a party hall that would attract customers of all ages; that did not seem very childish or something only attractive to adults. After thinking and thinking, we came up with the idea that the main attraction at our party hall would be a mechanical bull. Yeehaw! Never in our lives had we ridden one; however, they seem to be a ton of fun, so that's what we agreed on.

My wife and I took on the task of researching mechanical bulls. We realized that there were very few companies in the United States that manufacture mechanical bulls. Talking to some of these companies, we also discovered which were the important features that we needed to consider when making the purchase.

First, mechanical bulls are considered amusement rides, so they could be dangerous. This means that you cannot just buy any bull, but you have to buy the best and with the best security features in the market. For the reason that it is considered an amusement ride, the cost of the insurance is through the roof. Second, be sure all the equipment—including control box, motor, and inflatable—is durable and of very good quality. Third, the idea of riding a mechanical bull is to have an experience that is the closest thing to riding a real bull, if that's what you want. The movement, the way it turns, and bucks are also very important. Especially in our case since we wanted something suitable for children, as well as adults. Finally, you want to find one with the appearance of a real bull.

After searching and comparing mechanical bulls for about a month, we found what we wanted—without a doubt, in our opinion, the best we had seen. It had everything we considered important. It could be ridden by both children and adults, with a twenty-by-twenty-foot inflatable mattress that was large enough so when riders fell off the bull, they would not get hurt. It had different speeds that went from very slow to advanced; its movements were so similar to those of a real bull that it could be used to train riders who rode bulls in competitions. It looked so real with horns and even cowhide; the control system and all the technical features were of great quality and quite sophisticated. My wife and me prayed, but our prayer was for God to bless our business. What I mean is that we made our plan for a business we wanted, but we had not consulted with God if that was what he wanted for us.

We found a company that was going to build a plaza with commercial spaces. We went to the bank first to see if we could get a loan for the business.

The bank required a business plan to know what the business consists of. Based on the details, they'd decide if we could get the loan. We did not know what a business plan was or how to put one together, so we sought help. We got in contact with an organization that supports small businesses in our area. We made an appointment with a business advisor who explained to us about the information we would need to prepare the business plan and how to do it. Now I understand why this requirement was so important. As the scripture says in Proverbs 29:18, "Where there is no vision, the people perish: but he that keepeth the law, happy is he," the business plan was to help and protect us. There were several banks that were not interested in the project. We looked for a type of government assistance and we applied, but we only qualified for a small percentage of what we were asking for, and we would have had no savings for the difference. Finally, we found a bank that approved the loan, although only 80 percent of the total we needed.

We made a blueprint of how we wanted the party hall and presented it to the contractor who was building the commercial plaza. The plaza was to the north of the city, in a highly trafficked area that was growing both in the commercial and residential areas. After several revisions to the contract, we reached an agreement. We paid the deposit to begin construction. Once we secured the premises, we then decided to purchase the mechanical bull since it took approximately two months for it to be manufactured and shipped from Pennsylvania. The mechanical bull had a price tag of $22,000, but they could start manufacturing it with 50 percent down payment, and the rest we could finance.

The construction of the premises was progressing as expected, very slowly. Finally, months later, the time came when the contractor told us that they would soon finish building so that we should start wrapping up the loan. At that time, my job was temporary; however, Tom, my supervisor, wanted me to work full-time for the company, so he was in contact with the human resources to offer me a full-time job and a new position. Then one day, Tom did not show up at work. Two weeks went by and I still had not heard from Tom. Human resources called me on a Friday to let me know it was my last day with the company; that Tom was not there to extend my contract, and that he was the only one who could. When my colleagues learned that it was my last day with the company, they were very upset. They advised me to leave all pending work hanging. Of course, I was not going to do that. I told them I couldn't; that I was grateful for the opportunity I had been given and wanted to leave the company in good terms. I wanted to be remembered for what I contributed to the company.

A few days later, Tom contacted me, apologizing for what had happened. He spoke to the utility company, and he was advised of my departure. He told me the reason for his absence; he had been hospitalized. He had had a test and had to have a liver biopsy. When he went to the hospital for a biopsy, his kidney was damaged during the procedure that he had to have an emergency surgery. By the time he awoke, it had already been a week. When Tom called me, he was still in the hospital. I went to visit him at the hospital and had the opportunity to pray for him. I prayed for a speedy recovery.

Once he improved a bit, he was transferred to a rehabilitation hospital, the same place I had been after the stroke. On one occasion, my wife accompanied me to visit him. When we arrived, she was so surprised that Tom was in the same room where I had been during my rehabilitation years before. Tom's wife was with him. When we entered the room, he was very happy to see us. I said, "You know, Tom, this was the same room where I was in when I was doing my rehabilitation and look at me, I am healed. I walked out of this place and just like I recovered, you, too, are going to recover." He smiled and gave us the bad news that the doctors had found liver cancer. I encouraged him by telling him that there was someone who could heal him and that he was going to heal him. Tom smiled. I asked if he would like us to pray for him, and he quickly said, "Yes, of course." We prayed for him, and he started telling my wife how his life had changed when he met me. He told my wife he had been asking God for an answer to his prayer and that I had given him that answer to his prayer. Tom's wife was very happy to have met me; she told us that Tom would speak to her about me. Then he told me that he was not going back to the company where we worked, and again, he apologized because I had been fired. In fact, he was very upset that he couldn't do anything else for me at the company.

Once Tom was discharged from the hospital, they decided to move back to Dallas for his treatments. Sometime later, he called me to give me the good news that the cancer had disappeared. I was very happy for him and said, "You see. There is someone who could heal you." He was so joyful because God had not only healed him physically but emotionally and spiritually too. I called him several times and sent him messages to see how he was doing, but after a few months he didn't answer or call me back. About two years later, Tom's wife called to let me know that Tom had passed away because of a heart attack. She told me that he would see my messages and missed calls, but his health was already very deteriorated, and he was not able to answer. She told me that even though our friendship was relatively short, Tom always remembered me with great affection and referred to me as "buddy." I thanked her for letting me know and prayed for her.

I went back to the bank to continue with the business-loan process. One of the questions in the application was about my employment status and had to disclose that I had been terminated. That changed everything in relation to the loan. We could no longer get the loan because I was now unemployed, and for a business to start bearing fruit, it takes time, at least six months. Without a job, I wouldn't have income to pay the loan. I left the bank very upset, and worried at the same time, since the building was almost finished, the mechanical bull had already been delivered, and we had contracts with both companies. We went to speak with the builder to tell him what had happened. To our surprise, he told us that there would be no problem; that the room had not been finished yet, and as for the deposit, he would have to speak with the owner of the premises. After a few days, he told us that the deposit would be refunded. To this day, we know that it was God who touched the heart of this man, but in returning the deposit, that was only God's grace. As for the mechanical bull, we had to keep it. We kept it in an empty room in the house. We didn't want to give up on the business and kept looking for other locations, but it didn't work. We decided to wait for a new job opportunity and start the business; however, I couldn't find a job. An experience that I, unfortunately, knew all too well.

After a year of having the mechanical bull put away, unopened, and making monthly payments on it of more than $500.00, we decided to rent it out for parties and social events. We didn't even know what we were getting into! First of all, even before we started renting it, we had to put it together. That's when we realized that the mechanical bull system had several components, large and quite heavy. You may think that we are wimps, but my wife and me could not set it up by ourselves. I remember the time we were finally able to set it up, it was so exciting. Although we realized that there were details that had to be adjusted and that we would need help, it was a great achievement for us. God opened doors. A neighbor lent us his trailer to be able to transport the mechanical bull system, and other neighbors helped us by assembling and operating Mr. Vill, the name we gave our mechanical bull. It was an adventure, but, oh boy, we did enjoy it.

The first rental we had was an event for our local church. It was a Mexican-themed event, so the mechanical bull fit in with the theme perfectly. The time of the party came, and we began to set up the system. We were a bit nervous because we wanted to provide excellent service and for people to have fun. And it was. The success was such that even our pastor rode it.

Right away, we looked for ways to assemble and disassemble the equipment in a faster and more efficient way. We went from taking an hour to set it up to only half an hour. Since then, we had great success. We had party after party, with very good results. There was never an issue with our customers. In fact, we had repeat customers. We liked that business so much because it gave us the opportunity to provide our customers and their guests with a fun experience.

After a little more than a year of renting the mechanical bull for social events and parties, the day came when God asked me to pass it on to some very dear friends. The exact words were, "It is time for my bull to be a blessing to the Hernandez's[3] as it has been

---

[3]   The Hernandez is a fictitious name to maintain the privacy of their identity.

to your family." And I, like every good Christian, knowledgeable in the word, began to rebuke that! I also questioned God. How are we to sell it when we are making profit? How are we to sell it when it cost us so much money? We weren't going to get back what we had invested. Besides, we really enjoyed the business. We were at a point where we had learned to handle it well and had established our clientele. I began to reason instead of obeying in faith. Not only that, God had already asked me to quit my job to spend more time with him and help more in the ministry. I ignored that too. I had not left the job nor passed the business to the Hernandez's. But as you may know, God does not need our approval when he wants to get something done, and that is a good thing. Well, that's what happened. Pretty much over-night, we no longer had reservations for the mechanical bull. Weird thing because we had already made ourselves well known in the area where we offered our service; the word had already spread that there was an amazing mechanical bull in the Rio Grande Valley, and on the website were very good comments from our customers. Then I remembered what God had already told me, and I was being disobedient.

In our couples' small group, there was a lady prophet of God. One night, after most of the couples had left, only we, the Hernandez family, my mother-in-law, and the prophet and her husband stayed. That night, God told them several things. One of those things was that he was going to give the brother a business; that it had nothing to do with what he did; when he was offered the business, it was not going to seem as if it was coming from God, but that was the business that God had for him. I had not told my wife what God had already told me about the mechanical bull, but that night, at the same time that God spoke to that couple through his prophet, God also spoke to my wife. At that moment, she knew that the business that God had for this man was the mechanical bull, but she did not mention that to me, just yet. My wife is very careful not to influence me when God is dealing with me.

The next morning, my wife asked me if God had told me anything. I already told you that my wife has a very generous heart, so God has used her several times to confirm what he has already told me. I said, "No." I know what you are thinking. Please don't judge me. I've repented since then. My wife, although I had not mentioned it, already knew that God had already told me about the mechanical bull, so she laughed and said, "Well, I think the business that God is going to give to that man is the mechanical bull." Several weeks went by and the mechanical bull had not moved. We didn't have any reservations at all.

Smiling, my wife asked me, "Has God told you anything about the mechanical bull?"

Again, I said, "No."

A few days later, still without reservations, my wife, with a hint of impatience in her tone, asked me, "When are you going to give the Hernandez's the mechanical bull?" I couldn't deny it anymore. I had to confess to my wife what God had told me. I felt as if a huge weight had been lifted off me. She was very pleased because she knew the longer we kept the bull, the longer we were in disobedience. She was sure that we should give them the mechanical bull, but God instructed me otherwise. I asked God how much and in what terms would we cut the deal with them. He told me to sell it with everything, including the trailer, which we had already purchased to transport the mechanical bull for less than half the amount we paid. God told me to tell them to pay me whenever they could and in any way they could. My jaw dropped, but I obeyed. A week later, we invited the Hernandez's to dinner at our house. They seemed a bit odd when they arrived at the house, as if they already knew that we were cooking up something. While we had dinner, I shared with them what God had put in our hearts. I offered them the mechanical bull and what God had said. The sister was very joyful. It took her husband a few seconds to process it. He appeared confused with the news that he even seemed to doubt. I told them that they didn't have to accept; that they could think about it, pray a few days, and then give us an answer. The sister, a woman of prayer and enormous faith, looked at her husband as if wanting to pinch him under the table so he would accept. (Remember, God had already told our brother that when the offer came, it would not seem like it came from God.) After a couple of minutes, the man accepted. They were delighted to know that God was answering their prayers.

A few months later, they brought us the first payment. I told them that it was not necessary. Although I had already obeyed God and left my job, my family and me were okay. We did not have wealth, but God was supplying all our needs. I told them that if they needed it, they could use it. However, this was something God had instructed them, and they were being obedient. After a few months, God asked me to forgive them the debt of the mechanical bull, so was the balance. Really? Again, I began to rebuke that thought. It could not be the voice of God since I had already been unemployed for months, and now, we needed the money. But it was the voice of God that spoke to me.

God spoke to my wife and me through a pastor at different places and on different occasions about grace. This pastor shared on how grace works. He gave an example of someone whose mailbox had been smashed by a careless driver crashing into it with their car. This pastor commented how justice would be to make the driver pay for the damages of the mailbox and the cost to replace it since it was because of his carelessness. However, grace would be to forgive the debt; that is, to tell the driver, "You don't owe me anything."

It reminds me of salvation. You see, we have all sinned and fell short of the glory of God. Not only that, but the wages/payments of sin—what we have earned for our sin—is death. God, being the loving and graceful Father that he is, sent his only begotten son, Jesus, to pay for our sin, removing our debt. He didn't have to do it; he chose to, granting us eternal life instead of eternal death. Jesus did the hard part on the cross; all we have to do is accept him. If you have not accepted Jesus in your heart, I invite you to do it wherever you are. Accept the gift of eternal life. (Please turn to page 105.)

That same week, we invited the couple to have coffee with us. There, we gave them the news. I told them that God loved them so much that they no longer had to pay me anything. The funny thing was that when we worked on the numbers, what we got back was 10 percent of everything we had invested in the mechanical bull. The mechanical bull was never mine but God's, and it was he who was generous with his children. We have only been stewards. Read the following verses that affirm this.

"The silver is Mine, and the gold is Mine," says the Lord of hosts. (Haggai 2:8 NKJV)

The earth is the Lord's, and all its fullness, the world and those who dwell therein. (Psalm 24:1 NKJV)

(Be a good steward. Remember that everything we have is his.)

Fisherman

Several years ago, the Lord told me that he would make me a great fisher of men. (Maybe that's why he used my wife to remind me as confirmation when he asked me to resign from my job.) Me, fisher of men? I couldn't even catch a fish in the water. It was when I understood that, just like it is difficult to fish for fish since it takes a lot of patience, so it is with man. I have learned that for a man to open up and talk about his emotions and struggles, one must share or open up first.

That happened to me in a small group at church. I noticed the men in the small group I led were very quiet at one point. At first, I didn't know what to do since I was the only one talking. It seemed as if I was the only one who had something to say.

I remember I was still taking the Next Level course, but I was now in the internship phase. During this phase, I was assigned a pastor for three hours a week to mentor me. The very next day, I realized what was happening with the group. I was to meet with my mentor. He always asked how I was doing and if there was anything he could do for me or how he could help me. I mentioned what was happening with my small group and how I felt to see that the men were not interacting. My mentor, Pastor Roland, gave me a book called *The Way of The Shepherd* by Dr. Kevin Leman and William Pentak for me to read. When I started reading the book, I realized how we should love others. As the scripture

says in Matthew 22:39, "A second is equally important: 'Love your neighbor as yourself.'"

(How much do you love yourself?)

The next week, when I met with the small
group again, I began sharing with them about the
teaching. I remember that it was about the tree of
the knowledge of good and evil. So I shared about
my testimony that I, having knowledge of what was
good, had been doing what was not good. Let me tell
you what happened.

I confessed that I had been addicted to pornog-
raphy for many years. I told them how Satan used
that to make me feel ashamed. That every time I fell,
I didn't want to approach God as a result of shame
after that. Also, that even while I was serving and
speaking of God, I was still doing what was wrong.

My wife realized that something was happening to me because my attitude began to change, but
I didn't want to confess anything because the first
time I had confessed, she was very upset, to say the
least. So out of guilt, condemnation, and fear of my
wife's reaction, I didn't want to confess. Nor did I
have the confidence to tell anyone else because I was
also afraid of being judged. Many things would come
to my mind. I remember one night that God told
me to confess my sin to my wife. I asked God, "Did
you not hear all that she said she would do to me if
I fell again?" I quickly realized that he heard because
he is omnipresent. I asked God to prepare my wife's

heart so that she would not be hurt. I built myself up with courage and confessed my sin to my wife. By this time, my wife already loved the Lord and consequently had a very different reaction from the first time. She responded with love and compassion toward me. She said to me, "I'm glad you told me because there is no one else, apart from God, who cares about your purity more than me." It was as if a ton of shame, lust, and guilt fell off me. Well, the scripture says in 1 John 1:9, "If we *confess our sins*, He is faithful and just to forgive us our sins and to cleanse us from all unrighteousness," (emphasis added). At that moment, I realized that even when I am tempted, even when I fall, I can the trust the One who lives in me.

*(Don't keep that sin in the dark with
you or it will eat you up.)*

Once I shared my testimony with the small group, one by one they began to open and share about what they were going through. Because I was able to be vulnerable, I gained the trust of each of them. I began to experience what it is to be a fisherman. The bait was my testimony. After that, it was just a matter of waiting for them to open up, and so it was.

I continued with the Next Level course. At the end of the first phase of the course, I was assigned the role of pastoral care coordinator. As such, I was responsible for coordinating baptisms, funerals, weddings, hospital visits, and praying for the congregation when necessary. Part of my responsibility was not only to coordinate the baptisms but also to form teams to help me with the preparations. I didn't know how I was going to do it since I had never formed teams before, but I was surprised to see that God already had all the people ready. God gave me favor to form the teams I needed to put together. Today, the church has three campuses, and each campus has its own baptism team.

There was also a need for a team to officiate funerals, so there was another opportunity to form another team. I sought my mentor for direction who advised me to contact the church pastors for information and ideas since they had previously officiated funerals. That is precisely what I did. I also gave myself the task of forming a team and training them as soon as possible so that they could officiate funerals. I only made the invitation to a few people. However, they spread the word overnight, and I had a team of twelve people ready to be trained. God can indeed multiply!

As the end of the first year of the Next Level–course approach, I told Ms. Libby, the course director, that it would be a good idea for this program to be offered in Spanish so that the members of the Spanish service also had the opportunity to grow spiritually and develop the calling that God has entrusted to them. I enjoyed the Next Level so much that I wanted it to be available to everyone. It was two years of intensive studies, growth, and blessings.

She told me she would think about it. Weeks later, she called me into her office. Ms. Libby told me that after thinking about it, Next Level in Spanish would be offered again since the first time it was offered, it had to be cancelled because of lack of interest. When she told me that the program would be offered in Spanish, I was filled with joy. She continued saying that I would coordinate the program, but she would support me and guide me. I froze. Of course, I wanted the Next Level to be offered, but I hadn't considered taking on that responsibility myself. I was very excited! After thinking about it for a bit, I accepted and got to work.

I started to invite people, and soon, I had fifteen people for the program. I told several of them how this program had helped me to grow and how opportunities opened up for me and my family as a result of obeying the voice of God. To my surprise, the word spread quickly. On the first day, more leaders than expected showed up committed to seek more from God and grow as leaders. Those two semesters, I was able to coordinate the program in Spanish and shepherd the sheep God had entrusted to me. The goal was achieved. At the end of the year of lessons, intensive studies, and projects, about half of these disciples graduated and half of them became interns in different ministries at church.

The Plans

———■———

There are times when it is difficult to understand God's plans and his timing. I don't know if it has ever happened to you, but I was one of those people who made plans and for one thing or another, they didn't work out as I expected. An example in the Bible about what I am trying to say is found in Mark 15:21, "A man named Simon, who was passing by but was from Cyrene, was coming from the field just then, and the soldiers forced him to carry the cross of Jesus. (Simon was the father of Alexander and Rufo.)" The scripture does not give many details, but when I read it, I imagined that Simon was on his way to his destination when he was forced to help Jesus carry the cross. I'm sure carrying the cross was the last thing Simon expected to do. At that moment, Simon probably thought, *What am I doing here? Why did I come this way?* Perhaps curiosity won him over. Like all humans, the scandal attracted him to see what was happening. As we read the story now, we think it was an honor for him to have carried the cross. This has happened before. I have a plan, but God has another, and with a cross included. My plan was always to be an expert in cyber security, but God called me to the ministry. We might think that our path is the best, but no matter how bad, difficult, or unusual it is, God's will is always the best for us.

(Just help, serve others, and God will reward you.)

Several years ago, we went to see a house that was being foreclosed, which means that it was on sale because the previous owners could no longer make their monthly payments. When we went to see it, we liked the lot and the location more than anything. The property was more than two acres, with many trees and on the outskirts of the city where we live. The house needed a few repairs. When we went to see it, we prayed for the house, and we asked God that if it was his will that he work a miracle so that we would be able to purchase that house. That house could be purchased through an auction; an offer could be made for an amount based on the value of the house. The house was for sale through HUD, which is a branch of the government which sells such houses. They were asking $150,000 for the house, which had three bedrooms, two bathrooms, plus two acres of land. We asked God to tell us how much to offer for the house. The Lord told me to offer $105,000, which was $45,000 less than what they were asking for. We contacted the realtor lady, who had shown us the house, to communicate our offer. She bluntly told us that they would not accept; that HUD never accepts such low offers, so she did not submit our offer. Let me tell you something. There are times when the Lord gives you a word, and it seems impossible because it has never happened before. Let God make history with what he wants to do with you and through you. After all, with God, everything is possible.

We immediately looked for another realtor to make the offer. Once we had made the offer, several weeks went by, but we did not have an answer. We kept praying for the house and for HUD to accept the offer. One day, God told me, "Because your wife doubted, they will not accept the offer. Offer $110,000. They will take $110,000." A few days later, they rejected our offer of $105,000.

Our second offer was $110,000. Time went by. The days turned into weeks, and weeks turned into months until about three months later, we received an answer. They accepted $110,000, just as God had said; something that HUD didn't do regularly. Even our realtor was surprised the offer was accepted. By this time, we had already been working with a mortgage loan officer. The mortgage loan had already been preapproved, but since we had a ton of debt, ended up being denied. I became angry. The first thing that came to mind was, *This is exactly the same thing that happened with the business.* But that was not true. God told us how much to offer for the house, and so it was.

We were wondering what had happened, or what God wanted to show us with these two experiences, the business and the house. About a year later,

God spoke to us through a prophet who told us that we should not take roots here because God would move us from here.

In those two situations, the house and the business deals had gone south, yet we saw the supernatural power and grace of God in an extraordinary way. We know that he listens and continues to listen to our prayers as the Word says in 1 John 5:14, "Now this is the confidence that we have in Him, that if we ask anything according to His will, He hears us."

Now I believe that if we had the business and house, we would be stressed out and worried about the mortgage and rent for the business. We might even be blaming God for giving us the business and the house. He showed us he is good and listens to our prayers.

(Don't lose faith. Persevere and keep trusting because rain is coming soon.)

We now know that our promised land is north of us, and we believe it is in the Dallas area. So every now and then, my wife looks for houses that are for sale in that area. Two months before our twentieth wedding anniversary, my wife saw a house in a city on the outskirts of Dallas that she liked very much. She told me that when she was looking for houses online, she saw that house, but it was so beautiful and quite expensive that she didn't even dare to click the link to see the photos. A few days later, she kept on looking for houses in that area and saw that house again. This time, she felt like something from the inside her was telling her to click the link to see the photos and the description of the house. She tells me that when she clicked to see the photos, she could not contain herself and exclaimed out loud, "Lord, I love it!" as if it were something God was showing her.

We talked to Marlon, our youngest son, since Yair, our eldest son, was out of town, visiting a university. Remember I told you that Marlon has a faith that moves mountains? My child's faith never ceases to amaze us. When he saw the photos, he liked the house very much and began to pray. He started telling us that we could have small groups at the new house, and that as soon as we move, he will start his small group there as well. (He currently leads a small group here with boys his age and younger.) His faith is such that he even began packing his clothes, toys, and blankets. Since then, he has been praying and asking God for the new house, the promised land, small groups, two Rottweilers, and a rabbit. Every day he asks me, "Daddy, are we almost moving to the promised land and the new house?" His faith is so contagious that we also began to pack a few things.

About a month after my wife saw the house for the first time, we saw a preaching by Pastor Michael Todd of Transformation Church in Tulsa, Oklahoma. In that sermon called "Crazy Faith," he shares his testimony about what God spoke to him; that a very large building in the city would become Transformation Church; that is, God would give him that building for his church. He says that he then visited the building, knowing that it was greater than what he could achieve with his own strengths or abilities, but trusting in what God had said. During the sermon, he shared the video he had recorded five years ago—it was his testimony of crazy faith—and it is now a reality since they have now purchased the building for his church. The video was so touching that God challenged me. He dared me to go to Dallas with my family and do the same thing so that, when the time comes, I will also use the video to give him glory. A week later, we went to Dallas to shoot our "crazy faith" video at that house.

Anniversary Gifts

As you know, my wife and me have just celebrated twenty years of marriage. For our eighteenth wedding anniversary, God gave us an anniversary gift. I know there are people to whom God gives them something special for their birthday, but for us, it has been our anniversary.

Marlon, our youngest, was diagnosed with hemihypertrophy when he was only five months. This condition causes one side of the body to grow faster than the other. In our son's case, the left side of his body grew faster. When he was diagnosed, it was very difficult for us because, as parents, one wishes and prays for healthy children. Also, with this condition, the risk of childhood cancer in the abdominal organs increases.

Consequently, since he was diagnosed, it was necessary for ultrasounds to be performed on our baby while fasting. Since I was unemployed, I was the one who took him to his medical appointments and studies. When our baby had appointments, my wife would call me on the phone, and I would tell her how we were doing. Our baby, like most babies, was very hungry in the morning, and waiting on an empty stomach to have an ultrasound was like torture for him. This would break my wife's heart, knowing that our baby was very hungry every time he had to get an ultrasound.

We would pray together for his healing, but one day, while Marlon was still a baby, my wife made a covenant with God. She told God that we would no longer take our baby to get ultrasounds but he had to heal Marlon; that she would trust him for the healing of our son. And so it was for several years; no more ultrasounds. We would only take him to his routine appointments to see how he was growing.

At the age of six or seven, Marlon began complaining of a stomach pain. We prayed and made a few changes to his diet, but he did not improve, so we took him to the doctor for a checkup. The doctor ordered an ultrasound, just what my wife had promised God we would no longer do to Marlon. It was very difficult for her, but she agreed to it. The results showed that our son was fine; there was nothing to be concerned about.

The routine checkups were to assess how Marlon was developing, especially his legs since the difference in the length of his legs could cause complications, not only when walking, but also to his spine. The difference between his left and right leg became a little more than an inch. We never mentioned to our son about the condition he had been diagnosed with since we didn't want him to feel limited or incapacitated in any way. Besides, God gave

Marlon the ability to walk on tiptoes, so there was no abnormality when walking. In fact, in the fourth grade, he competed in track and won second place. He had, and still has, a totally normal life.

It was not until the age of ten, a few weeks before our eighteenth wedding anniversary; that Marlon began with a pain in his leg. The pain continued for a few days, and then he began to limp. He had never limped before, so it was very hard for us, especially for my wife. My wife examined him to see if the difference in length between his legs had increased and, at first glance it seemed as it had, a little. We continued praying for his complete healing. My wife cried out to God for the health of our son more than ever before.

A few days later, as he continued with pain and limping, he realized on his own that he had one leg that was longer than the other. One day, after school, he casually shared his findings regarding his leg with us. He told us that this was the cause of the pain in his leg. We had to explain the doctors' diagnosis to him, but we also let him know that we were still trusting that God could heal him completely.

The night before our eighteenth anniversary, I was already in bed, when I heard God tell me, "It is done. Marlon is healed. I'm not a man to lie." I told my wife, and she started crying with joy and gratitude, but also because she felt as if she had failed God. As it was late at night, we didn't want to wake Marlon up. The next day, my wife asked our son to show her the "short leg" as he had named his right leg. Marlon stood in front of my wife and looked at his feet, moving from side to side, putting his weight first on one and then on the other, and said with a smile on his face, "It's gone!" Yes, the short leg was gone. What a joy! God literally stretched my son's leg so that his legs would be even. Not only that, he stretched his arm as well. Since he had been diagnosed, we prayed for his complete healing, including his physical healing. But it was until our eighteenth wedding anniversary that his healing was physically manifested. What an amazing anniversary gift!

Since then, my wife expects an anniversary gift from God. So for our nineteenth wedding anniversary, she was expecting a house or something like that. About a month before our anniversary, she told me that God was putting a number in her heart and that she knew that he wanted that number to be the percentage of income that we would return to the kingdom. Let me explain.

Several years ago, our church played a video of Pastor Rick Warren's testimony on generosity. He shared how since they got married, he and his wife, Kay, decided to increase the percentage of income returned to the kingdom each year. The Bible teaches us how to tithe, or return 10 percent of your income to God which belongs to him. Rick Warren and his wife increased their percentage every year as the Lord prospered them. When we watched the video, they were returning 90 percent of their income to the kingdom of God. My wife quickly told me, "I want to do that!" We prayed and decided to increase 2 percent, to return 12 percent to church.

We did so for a while until I found myself in a tight spot and, without consulting my wife, decided to subtract 1 percent. Soon, our finances began to suffer tremendously. I started praying to God and asking him to help us. He was the one who reminded me of what we had promised—12 percent, not eleven. God is so good; he didn't throw it in my face or demand it. He simply reminded me to bless us. So we went back to 12 percent.

Little by little, we reached 16 percent. By this time, he told me to put that additional percentage into a Jewish ministry, and that is what we have done since then.

Now returning to the anniversary gift. The number that God was putting in my wife's heart was twenty. To reach that percentage, we would have to increase 4 percent apart from what we were already returning to the kingdom. At that time, our finances were already in a critical state; we had almost exhausted what we had in our stockpile, and I was still unemployed. My wife told me that she was sure that if we obeyed, that God would open a door for me to work at the church since everything indicated that God only wanted me to work for him and no one else.

Although it was not easy, we obeyed. God continued to work with us, our priorities, and trust in him. Our budget was in red numbers every two weeks. But every two weeks, we saw God miraculously provide everything we needed and make our payments. How could he disappoint us? We were doing our part. Eight months later, I was offered a job at the church. It was part-time, but I knew it was where God wanted me to be, working for him.

So for our twentieth wedding anniversary, we no longer knew what to expect, but we knew we would have a gift from God, and so it was. Weeks before our twentieth anniversary, my wife and me decided to take a finance class online. The class is offered by Gateway Church and is called Financial Hope Workshop. This workshop consists of seven classes, one per week. We knew that God was going to do something in relation to our finances as he says in Malachi 3:10:

> Bring all the tithes into the storehouse, That there may be food in My house, And try Me now in this," Says the Lord of hosts, "If I will not open for you the windows of heaven And pour out for you such blessing That there will not be room enough to receive it.

(If we just return of what is his, he will open the floodgates of heaven.)

We have been faithful in our tithes and offerings for years, but we had not been good stewards in our finances. The workshop helped us to do that: worship God even with the way we use finances. So we started by learning to keep track of our expenses, all of them, since that would be the way we could know where the money was going. We realized where we were spending money unwisely, and that we were being careless with what God had placed in our hands. We learned that stewardship is so important, not only in our finances, but in all aspects of our lives. We also learned how to prepare a budget, to eliminate our debt, and how long it would take to achieve it. It was quite encouraging. *By the way, if you have never taken a stewardship class, I recommend this workshop.* We also learned the importance of saving for our future, but most importantly, it became clear to us that God is the owner of everything, and that we are only stewards. In the end, we are not going to take anything when we leave this world.

From the first class, we received a truth and promise from God; this was that if we did what we could do to improve our finances, God would do what we could not do. We prayed that it would be so in our lives. That same week, after starting the workshop, I met with my pastor for my job evaluation. It went great; he told me that they were very happy with me; that my work was a blessing for the church; and therefore, they wanted to offer me a full-time job.

The day after our twentieth anniversary, which also happened to be the last day of the course, Ms. Libby, who also happens to be the church administrator, called me to her office to officially offer me full-time job. I also got a salary increase. I believe God was willing to bless us in such a way because he knew that we had been faithful and good stewards when in lack; therefore, he could increase our resources. Well, the scripture says in Matthew 25:23, "His lord said to him, 'Well done, good and faithful servant; you have been faithful over a few things, I will make you ruler over many things. Enter into the joy of your lord.'" Seeing God's faithfulness so palpable in our lives has been beautiful; seeing it in our finances has been a relief.

(Be faithful in the little, and you will see his power and favor over you.)

My Calling

———————■———————

Years ago, God gave me a dream. In that dream, I was preaching in a big building, like a big church. I remember the dream well because people were being healed of all kinds of diseases. There was even someone in a wheelchair. When I saw her, I asked her to get up in the name of Jesus. The lady stood up and began to walk. Not only had she regained strength in her legs, but she had also been healed of all the diseases she suffered.

I woke up that day very happy to know that God was going to use me to heal people. As time went by, I prayed, and people were healed. There was one day that my wife and me were reminiscing about this dream. My wife reminded me that the first time I had that dream was twenty years ago, when we were newlyweds. My wife started telling me about what happened that morning.

At that time, we lived in a small one-bedroom apartment. It wasn't even furnished. She was still in her senior year of high school. When I woke up, I told her that I had had a somewhat odd dream. I told her that I saw myself in front of many people in a church, and that I was the one who spoke to them. Then she told me, "You cannot be a priest since we are already married." I explained to her that in my dream, I was a pastor, and that a pastor could be married. Well, we both didn't understand much since we had never set foot in a Christian church before. In truth, I did not give much importance to the dream because at that time, I did not know that God spoke to me through dreams or about the plans he has for me. As I spoke about before, we began to have marital problems, and I had a stroke where I heard God's voice. I met Jesus and began to serve him.

You know, we've all been through difficulties, and sometimes, even disappointments. However, these experiences have helped us both, to form our character and to grow spiritually. I have learned that when God does not answer our prayers, it is because our request will either not be a blessing or his timing or because he has something even better than what we are asking.

> But as it is written: "Eye has not seen, nor ear heard, Nor have entered into the heart of man The things which God has prepared for those who love Him."
> (1 Corinthians 2:9)

(You will see his heart in everything he has done.)

Remember the twentieth wedding anniversary gift from God—a change in our finances due to the full-time job offer and salary increase? When I talked to my wife, we were happy about the news. But there was an issue, so we started asking God if that was really what he wanted for us, especially for me. As I told you, the Lord has given me dreams where I am preaching to many people, and they are being healed. Likewise, God has told me that he would make me a great fisher of men.

The day Ms. Libby offered me the full-time job, it was bittersweet. Have you ever been there? You're expecting something, and when you get it, it's not quite the way you expected. I felt as if it was not what God had called me to do. I was afraid that by accepting the full-time job, I would be procrastinating the call that God has on my life, for my talent and knowledge in technology. Two months before I was offered the full-time position, God had told me that I would oversee the technology department at the church. When he told me, I was happy because it is something I like to do and what I went to school for. But when I was offered the position, it was bittersweet.

I had the idea that I was going to start moving toward my calling already. I was even sure that God had been preparing me. When I was taking the Next Level course, I realized that I had other qualities to help in the ministry that I didn't even know I had, but God had already put it in me, and I loved it. I told Ms. Libby that I was going to pray and then get back to her.

The next day, I began to pray. I asked God to speak to me and tell me what to do, if that is what he wanted for me, to tell me. While I prayed, he answered. His answer was, "Take the job, love it, and enjoy it." So I did.

We continued to trust that God will fulfill what he had promised at the perfect time. For the scripture clearly says in Romans 11:29, "For the gifts and the calling of God are irrevocable." At the moment, we continued to enjoy the place where he had planted us and what he had given us. We, my family and me, continued serving at the local church, which we loved. We know that his plans are better than ours.

(If you don't know your gift, just ask God. He will reveal it to you in Jesus' name, amen.)

A Final Thought

As I told you at the beginning of this book, God had not only given me the dream of writing this book, but he asked that I do it to bring hope to those who no longer have hope. There were times when I thought about giving up on this book because, as I told you, there was a time where I didn't feel like writing, and I thought that it was not going to be done. But God does not forget the promises he had made to us and reminded me again about the book. Through pastors who preached about how obedience to God brings blessings while disobedience could bring curse to our lives, I had a wake-up call that made me change and ask him for help. My prayer was that I would do the possible—sit down and write—and he did the impossible: guided my writing.

Let me remind you that you, like me, have been chosen by God for something, whether you know it or not. Do you realize that? Everything I've shared in this book has happened before I got where I'm going and did what he called me to do. Everything I've shared has happened on the way to the promise.

If you have been waiting on the Lord and on his promise, do not be discouraged. I am sure that you have also been chosen despite your limitations and, like me, you need a God greater than you to make that promise or promises a reality in your life.

> *I would have fainted*, if I had not believed that I would see the goodness of the Lord in the land of the living. (Psalm 27:13, emphasis added)

The reason I was able finish this book is because I believed that I would see his goodness here on this earth. So I encourage you, do not give up on your dreams; just wait for God. He will come through.

(His promises still stands. He is faithful.)

The Lord has been so good to me. I personally hope this book will help you in some way, not only in your spiritual life, but in your personal life, with your marriage, children, and finances. He is faithful with his promises. As you read the book, you have noticed how faithful he has been in my life, to me, my wife, and my kids, and that is just part of my life. I can't imagine what else he has planned for me. In the same way, my desire is that you find in this the answer that you were looking for. I recently heard a pastor share how God sent her to another city, where she didn't know anyone. Once there she met another lady, and they began talking. She didn't know what to talk about, but the Holy Spirit took her there just to meet with her. She was able to minister to her about questions she had through her own testimony. In the same way, I pray this book might have answers to your own prayers. I may not be physically with you to tell you how much Jesus loves you and that he is waiting for you, just like I did with Tom back then. This book has purpose, hope, and an encouraging message that you might need. Life is not easy, but once God reveals to you his purpose in your life, you will start to praise him like crazy, just like King David did. We live in a fallen world, but we don't have to quit our dreams and promises with the first storm or when the wind blows. He has given us a spirit of courage. God has a purpose for your life, and he knows exactly what you need. All you need to do is put your faith in him, and he will do the rest. All things are possible when we believe.

Prayer For You

God, thank you for this amazing day. Lord, I ask you for those that read this book. Lord, please reveal your purpose in them, help them to not be dismayed, and always put their faith in Jesus. Even when the storms come and the winds blow, keep them safe. May the Lord bless you and keep you. May his favor be upon you and be gracious to you. May the Lord provide you with everything that you need. May the Lord protect you in your coming and going. The Lord will open doors that man can't shut. And the peace that surpasses all understanding will be upon you. Amen!

Special Acknowledgments

———————●———————

Writing this book was harder than I thought and more rewarding than I could have ever imagined. None of this would have been possible without my friends and mentors. A special thanks to Pastor Bob and Libby Ordeman, for taking the time to read my rough draft and their advices. Eternally grateful to Patsy Muñiz, for helping me edit this book and her suggestions regarding the content.

I want to thank my awesome wife, Yendi. She was as important to this book getting done as I was. She is like the virtuous woman the Bible describes in Proverbs 31:25–29 (NLT).

> She is clothed with strength and dignity, and she laughs without fear of the future. When she speaks, her words are wise, and she gives instructions with kindness. She carefully watches everything in her household and suffers nothing from laziness.

Her children stand and
bless her. Her husband praises
her: "There are many virtuous
and capable women in the world,
but you surpass them all!"

With much love to my virtuous wife! I love you,
Yendi. You always understand what I might be going
through; you know how to respond and what to say
to lift my spirit. You are my cheerleader. I thank God
for putting you in my path and now sharing this
beautiful love story. Thank you for never giving up.
I love you!

*(Amazing love. God you are so good
for the woman you gave me.)*

Salvation Prayer

If you would like to make Jesus the Lord of your life, please say this prayer:

Father, I know that I have broken your laws, and my sin has separated me from you. I'm really sorry, and now I want to get away from my sinful life and turn to you. Forgive me. I believe that your son, Jesus Christ, died for my sins, rose from the dead, is alive, and hears my prayer. I invite Jesus to become the Lord of my life, to rule and reign in my heart from this day forward. Please send your Holy Spirit to help me obey you and do your will for the rest of my life. In the name of Jesus, I pray, amen.

About the Author

Milton Villarreal is the founder of Let's Pray Twogether, a bilingual ministry dedicated to pray for the needs of the public and America. He and his wife, Yendi Villarreal, have known each other since they were children and have just celebrated twenty years of marriage. They have two sons and have dedicated themselves to instruct them in the way of the Lord so that even when they are old, the would not depart from it. Milton gave his life to Christ in 2006. That year, Milton had a stroke that almost cost him his life. The same day when he suffered the stroke, he heard the voice of God for the first time. Since then, Milton decided to serve the Lord. Today, he is working at the church where he received Jesus as his savior. God has put in Milton's heart to write this book.

CPSIA information can be obtained
at www.ICGtesting.com
Printed in the USA
BVHW032142180821
614757BV00001B/10

9 781636 307176